Bartram's Garden

Books by Eleanor Stanford

Poetry
The Book of Sleep
Bartram's Garden

Nonfiction
História, História

Bartram's Garden

Eleanor Stanford

Carnegie Mellon University Press
Pittsburgh 2015

Acknowledgments

Thanks to the following journals where these poems have appeared:

American Journal of Nursing: "Alzheimer's Pantoum"
Bellingham Review: "The Apiary"
Harvard Review: "At the Steel Pier"
Ploughshares: "Bartram's Garden"
Poetry: "On a Line by Petrarch"
Folio: "The Poem I Meant to Write"
Indiana Review: "South Dakota Ghazal"
Drunken Boat: "Two Common Daffodils (*Narcissus pseudonarcissus*)"
Quarter After Eight: "Itapuã: Footnotes"
Quarterly West: "Agua de Beber," Invention of the Moon," "Windows"
Connotations Press: "Letter to Laura from Arembepe," "Brazil, Imaginary
    Island"
No Tell Motel: "Letdown," "Children," "Weaning," "Cashew," "Brava,
    fogo, corpo, lua"
New Collage: "Driving to the Shore with My Father," "I'm held by
    nothing, I hold onto nothing, I belong to nothing."
Noon: "Domestic"

"Urban Renewal" won first place in the Anna David Rosenberg Award.
"The Mangrove," "Parsnips," and "Invention for Cavaquinho and Pedal
    Steel" won the 2008 Dorothy Rosenberg Award.
"Dawn Redwood," "Smoothleaf Elm" and "Harvest: Midsummer" won
    the 2012 Dorothy Rosenberg Award.

Cover image: *Franklinia alatamaha, franklinia,* Drawing 1 (Ewan
Frontispiece) from the botanitcal and zoological drawings by William
Bartram (1756-1788), © The Trustees of the Natural History Museum,
London

Book design by Hannah Dellabella

Library of Congress Control Number 2014943692
ISBN 978-0-88748-598-5

10 9 8 7 6 5 4 3 2 1

Contents

4. The Vegetable Plot

5. The River Trail

The Nursery

The Apiary

I fit the walls in place with pliers,
hold them till the glue dries. The saw
hums, dust swarms and beats it wings
around my shoulders.

> All this dark summer I placed frame
> on frame. From my childhood I remember
> nothing. But my sons hang from the metal
> bars, unfold their bodies, mise en abyme.

Humidity swells the joints. Don't tell me
I've never built anything. I assembled these
cell walls from spit and pulp, I carried
the daub and wattle hive for months.

> The sunflowers bow their heavy heads,
> goldfinches shaking the stalks, bright yellow
> messengers of sorrow: their small flesh
> the smoke of old coal plants.

> We wed in a field: clover and wild carrot,
> and the veil obscuring my view. For a moment
> I was both queen and keeper, until the hum
> began—warning song, epithalamium.

Thich Nhat Hanh says do not ask,
Cloud, when were you born?
Deep hive body, brood chamber:
inside each box, another box.

      I stretch the wire across the wood;
      pull it taut to my thumb's callus.
      In the yard, the morning glory clings to the trellis,
      its blue stars squinting.

At the Steel Pier

The boardwalk creaks between
Trump Castle and the dark
Atlantic. I strap my son into
a rickety motorcycle ride,
then stand behind the gate
and watch his face:
the fear, the heartbreaking
three-year-old intensity.
I want to take him back
into my body: tide-swell
I followed only as far
as the black swirls of birth-slick hair.
The teenager operating the ride
removes his foot from the pedal,
it clanks and jolts
and stops at last. Unbuckled, my son
is running toward me,
proud and shaken. Behind us
the Ferris wheel spins,
seats swinging on its spokes
of light. How I held him then.
How I gripped the bed's chrome bar.

Urban Renewal

1.
In the rowhouse gardens, we keep to ourselves
among the mulch and potted basil.
Nothing grows from this soil but bleeding heart.

On the corner, the crossing guard in her fluorescent vest
gestures. She waves us on: the baby strapped sleeping
to my chest, schoolchildren with white shirttails
untucked, the azaleas' crumpled faces.

Opening the window today, my thumb
pushed through the pane.
It's a myth that glass is liquid.

We pour ourselves into whatever container
we can find.

2.
In prelapsarian Brooklyn, my grandparents walk hand in hand
down Flatbush Avenue: my bubbe barelegged beneath her skirt,
my zaydee hatless.

Then the Angel with his flaming sword
ascends the subway stairs, come
to lead them to a split-level on Long Island.

3.
Did her baby, too, play tricks,
red peony of his skull opening
on the sidewalk and her
helpless before its beauty?

4.
Milky scrawl across the sheets, invisible ink
missive. I express my grief into bottles,
let him drink it down.

5.
What's written here will be
erased. Geographies on the baby's scalp,
and the plates shifting
underneath. We drift.

I hurl the baby against the shoals.
Whorled conch of his ear, mussels'
fleshy interior.

6.
This is another way
I lie. I make it lovely.

7.
The fox glides in on his shadow,
waits at the edge of the playground.
The mother acknowledges him, lets him
lick the grape jelly from her fingers.

See, she says to the children. Invites them
to stroke the soft burnt fur
of her own fear.

The woods stitch up the city's ragged seam.

It imaged not amiss the moral wilderness
in which she had so long been wandering.

8.
But even Hawthorne's woods
did not exist, New England long since
turned to fuel and pasture.

History's the only wilderness.

Still, the woods return.

9.
The woods return, but there is no more wilderness.

The old Indian perched above Forbidden Drive
looks down on us with his stone face.
The ducks eat the Wonder Bread we throw them.

The woods will take the city back.
There's no more moral wilderness,
but still I refuse the antidepressants
the therapist doles out.

10.
Down the street, the peach tree's in full leaf—
the fruit unfleshed, all stone.
In the bassinet, the baby grunts and sighs.
Once, in a different city, I watched a legless man
play *mornas* on the violin.
Now that I've forgotten the language,
I begin to understand the song.

11.
Summer hits us in a sudden downpour.
There's no more wilderness
than this. In the yard the poppies flare
and hiss, extinguish.

Letdown

The baby cries, but worse
is waiting. Small breath
lifts the leaves.

Hand over hand, sap
descends the knotted rope.

In the yard, the chickens follow their traveling coop,
pecking the ground clean.

Brava, fogo, corpo, lua
after Mina Loy

I lived in my head.
Two years, the moon coming and going
over Brava and the volcano.
Another island in our pathetic
archipelago.

Every night I watched it rise over the island
whose name means brash, or angry, or foolhardy.
A rocky place we visited once, in a cold
and fog-draped March.

I lived in my head, my body could have grown wings
or shed itself in a dry husk, for all
I noticed.

I lived in my lantern.
Insects beat their flimsy wings around it.
My head
emitted a strange light.

Regret is intoxicating.
But once you've lost something, it's all
absurd. Marriage, children, funaná.
The boat's frenetic two-step, barrel's
empty rib.

I lived in my lantern. Outside, a goat licked
the island's moon-pocked cheek,
and young girls moved in and out of view
on the dirt road, carrying bundles of tinder on their heads.

Sete Portas, Salvador

1. Meningitis burns along the city's
curved spine, taillights on Otávio Mangabeira
extinguishing against the dark
salt-tongued Atlantic.

2. Feira de São Joaquim: the African women sit
impassive behind their stalls of dried beans,
bottles of hot *malagueta* peppers
preserved in oil, hung by the neck
from the rafters.

3. The knife provides another
ingress: passionfruit seeds spilling
on the counter, the orange's
sudden white-spoked wheel.

4. Or sleep: too little, too late, the baby teething,
the baby hot with fever, then morning,
pale dawn-colored door
slamming shut.

5. The bright colonial façades
hide dark rooms, ramshackle expanse
thick with squatters, men slouching
against the walls.

6. But how could we forget
the water? Bay of All Saints,
still harbor. The boys with their shiny bodies
diving from the pier.

7. Then again, the sky. So blue
those days when I bathed him
in the plastic tub outside, parted
his hair, let him call me mama.

Agua de Beber

Eu quis amar mais tive medo—

When my little ones were sick with fever,
and would drink only the sweet, cloudy
water from coconuts, Dete stood in the kitchen
with a machete and hacked them
open. Santa Clara, patron saint
of the local aquifer, where now
Monsanto washes runoff
over the permeable
rock—is this how it feels?
When the baby wouldn't take
even the milk I'd spun
from sunlight and black coffee, filtered
through my own good blood?
To calm myself, I palmed the cracked
green globe. When Dete was young
in the countryside, she said,
there were no doctors. Children died
from such simple things.
Meu interior, she called it, or equally,
a fora: the exterior. She scooped the quivering,
translucent flesh from the hard shell.

Children

They hollow you out. Their colored plastic shovels
working, scraping the bottom
of the sandbox.

Still, you can't say it.

What are you doing? I ask my two-year-old.
My back turned, stirring something.
Playing with knives, he says. His enunciation
newly honed, proud blade.

Look out the window. The suburbs' orderly
paved quiet. The streets named for tribes
long since extinct.

Last week, when I left
a bone-handled knife on the stove,
and the flame caught, I stood there, mouthing
Fire. Fire. As though saying it
I'd set the house ablaze.

Flora

Bartram's Garden

I.

What appears untidy and lacking
in design is in fact intentional:
quiet milkweed beside the conflagration
of red fireweed; the brackish
Schuylkill feeding stately oaks. John knew the author
lays his borders, then steps back. General
Washington, strolling the overgrown river trail,
pursed his lips; what sort of father
lets his seed run wild, allows entanglements
between sweetspire and the common daisy?
What man sends his son into the mazy
swamps of Georgia with no instruments
but a magnifying glass and quill,
to gather specimens of sweet gum, ash, and jonquil?

II.

Perhaps there is not any part of creation, within the reach of our observations, which exhibits a more glorious display of the Almighty Hand, than the vegetable world.

—William Bartram

It was William's hand, though, that dug up
the tea plant from beside the Altamaha
River, that wrapped the roots in wet burlap
and carried it home to Philadelphia.
His father, transplanting it in the silty soil
of the English colony, named it
for Ben Franklin. Franklinia boiled
in the nation's pots, blossoms a balm, thin
stalks a poultice. In Georgia, though,
the plant's leaves furled and fell off, gathered
on the ground like cut-out tongues. The Seminoles
took note, eradicated another
name from their lexicon. On a northern bank,
miles from extinction, the righteous botanist gave thanks.

III.
When he was read out of Quaker Meeting,
John went and sat among his cup plants
and coneflowers and watched a humming-
bird hover in the blurred outline
of its body. In the dovecote, those birds
gossiped in their gray language. From the kitchen
garden, he heard the feathered rustle of skirts,
his wife tending the small patch
of thyme and lavender. All exile,
he told himself, is temporary. It's true,
much later the Quakers would extol
his virtues, would boycott war and grapes and rue
their own intolerance. In flocks they'd tour
the grounds, house and gardens faithfully restored.

Tree of Heaven (*Ailanthus altissima*)

What is this punishment that glitters so?

—Dante's *Inferno*

Radiology gives me a paper gown
and a paper sash. A small cubby
in which to stow my clothes.

Outside the window,
the tree of heaven
flashes its dark belled sleeves,
its kimono of light.
The heart-shaped scars
along the trunk.

In China, silkworms chew
the toothless leaves,
spin them into an incandescent
filaments.

Here, though, the tree's
invasive. Or as they used to say: *exotic.*

The nurse calls my name,
and I press my chest against
the machine. On the screen,
a globe lit up. Intimate city.
Unfamiliar map of home;
atlas of what's to come.
And the remote islands
dying in the Pacific.

Red Horsechestnut (*Aesculus x carnea*)

The Orthodox women with their cheap wigs
and expensive strollers block traffic
from Union to Highland. Smug

with their large broods and the epigraphic
word of God. (Or maybe I'm projecting.)
Even though it's not my demographic,

some days I long to throw off my self-protecting
sneer, my tank top and my flip-flops,
to cover my ankles like any self-respecting

ima, to pin *yarmulkes* and Yiddish names atop
my sons' unsuspecting heads. Instead
I take them to the arboretum where we drop

coins into the fountain. Instead
I walk among the old trees. Summer
is one thing—forgiving, honey-lit.

But come fall, the sky gone glummer,
in the blank space of the high holy days,
formless longing thrums and murmurs:

palmate rebuke of the red horsechestnut
that drops its glossy spineless fruit.

Smoothleaf Elm (*Ulmus minor*)

The chemo leaves my mother
weak and docile, out
of sorts. Her head wrapped
in old scrap fabric, a garland
of tiny flowers.
But how young
she looks, the gray
erased, her eyes the pale green
of new leaves.

Invention for Vuvuzela
and Trumpet Flower

On the tiny screen in the guard's shack, the footballers
move like insects, animated by the buzzing timbral of the plastic
        horns.
Behind us the whole country is resplendent in green
and yellow—June's first corn in the interior, glossy-leaved,
silk-tongued. Little girls with green and yellow ribbons in their hair.
The rain last night was like a hundred hands
                                on a tinny piano.
A technical exercise,
                    a practice in transformations.
By the pool, the bell-shaped flowers
droop, beaded with rain.

The announcers' language is fast, full of trills
and small embellishments. This way
we practice evasion and control. This way we learn
and relearn the score.

João, who guards the door, leans back in his chair and watches
with his eyes closed.

Cashew

The dust blew in, covered our sheets.
We barely touched. Is dust
a season? Or the absence
of rain? We touched
infrequently, but you brought me
fruit, cradled in the hem of your t-shirt.

*

The apple clings to the nut's
hard shell, the flesh stringy
and astringent. Djidja taught us
how to crack them,
to extract the meat without touching
the poisonous resin that surrounds it.

*

Anacardium occidentale: Far Eastern
Heart. Is it the drupe—its muscled
blush—or the seed's hidden
aortal curve?

*

In Portuguese its name might mean
tangled skein. But it wasn't Portuguese

we spoke. What we learned
was something else: rough-skinned
and elliptical, at once newer
and more primitive.

*

Above the branch, the moth's
white-paned wings are marked
with eyes.

No. Don't call them eyes.

*

We picked more than we could eat.
The fruit, unsuitable
for transport, rotted on the ground.
We ate until our bellies ached.

*

And now the bell-shaped emptiness
ringing on my tongue. Its tannic
sting. We ate until
the trees were bare,
until the fruit was gone.

Ultrasound

1.
Summer again, the trees
have fleshed the idea of leaves
into leaves. At first it looks
formless, the technician says,
but the longer you look you begin
to see what's there. Kidney.
Spleen. The liver's silver lining.

How is it I have lived this long
without loss?

Still, the shadow of loss moves inside me.

I row out into its dark bay.

2.
On the other side of sound,
bone's shadow: beneath the acacia's ribbed
shade—rising, falling—I nursed the baby.

3.
Did you think it would be so easy
to remember? Or, for that matter,
so easy to forget?

I birthed my third son
in the bath. Beyond sound:
shadow mapping the water's
surface, small boat's ribbed
opening.

4.
I wrestled the slippery
vowels, mouthed
their fleshy fruit—cajú, cajá,
mamão—but nouns
were the easy part.
Each verb a dull knife,
the pronouns
slick dark seeds.

5.
Did you wonder where
they'd gone, those sounds you took
into your body, into even your
porous mosquito-netted sleep?

6.
This is where they congregate, then,
in the middle of my life, as in the evening
neighbors gathered beneath the trees to murmur
small endearments to the children,

to pinch their dusk-smoothed cheeks
and call them *delicious, pretty thing.*

7.
Unspoken-of desire: hair and gristle, toothed
and suety. Places where I won't live
again. Vestigial consonants I swallowed
for so many years.

8.
The heart is its own speciality, the technician says.
There it is, she says, but I can't tell you how
to read it.

9.
Accretion of bone
and cartilage, echo
in an empty
room. Small island
where I lived
at twenty-two, among
low-hanging clouds. Sometimes,
even through the fog, I could
make out the bougainvillea's
many-chambered hearts,
or the pulmonary swell
of sheep gliding past
the open window.

In Memoriam

Ezekiel Acorn
b. April 25, 2010 d. April 22, 2010

It was not the season of planting.
Still, we allowed ourselves small hope.

Just this: smooth nut a squirrel might
bury, not knowing from his putting by

comes growing. Rough cuplike base almost
umbilical, or—no—a little hat, exactly

what I would have knit—if I could knit—
to keep you warm.

Dawn Redwood

In dreams I return to Salvador. The roads
are washed out. I have to swim. Or
I am held at gunpoint
in front of the coconut stand.
Yet it is unmistakably
the same city where I once
lived. Where I walked
with a newborn in my arms,
first light spreading through the palms.
It is true, the dawn redwood,
believed to exist only as a fossil
was, in 1941, discovered living
in a rural Chinese province.
For myself, though, I do not believe
in miraculous returns.
In no region of this earth
will I again wake to soothe
an infant's ferny cries, or find myself
flooded, suddenly, with milk.

The Mangrove

I sit down on a wooden bench to nurse the baby
and the mosquitoes descend on their lithe legs.
His word for food is the same name
he calls me by: A-ma. A-ma.
The sharks circle in their small tank.

The blind drivers are guiding their Lexuses
down A1A and Spanish River.

My grandmother, who remembers little, recalls
telling the story of Passover to a preschool class.
Now we are free, she said, and one girl retorted,
No we are not. We are free and a half.

I can't sleep here, in this mutinous state, this brackish peninsula.
Dawn, dusk, the old people are out walking their small dogs
around the driveways of the complex. Beyond,
animals shelter in the mangal:

Peregrine falcon, American coot, rattlesnake.
Tangled food web of the intertidal zone. The baby's need
a drift net, cast wide and indiscriminate: tug of hunger
that catches at my breast.

Sea star. Propagule.
Black bee on a mangrove blossom.

When my grandmother woke
from the twilight sleep of giving birth, she saw
the nurses trying on her nightgowns, giggling.

The mangroves lift a lacy hem
of seafoam, their roots impenetrable.
Not two, not three.
We are free and a half. And each
elliptical leaf illuminated.

Fauna

Alzheimer's Pantoum

In the courtyard, a lizard suns itself.
It visits, silver-tongued, then leaves.
Why can't my husband stay with me?
I fear he has a second, hidden family.

He visits, silver-tongued, then leaves.
Dark girl with the singsong voice who bathes me—
is she my second, hidden family?
Her words are gentle, but her grip is fierce.

Dark girl with the singsong voice, who bathes me?
The water's black and glassy hand.
Its words are gentle, but its grip is fierce.
The drawbridge opens to let the boats pass through.

The water's black and glassy, a hand
mirror held to my cracked face.
The drawbridge opens to let the boats pass through—
tall spokes. No, that's wrong. Each word's

a mirror held to my cracked face.
My dark girl strokes the blush across my cheek.
Tall soft-spoken girl, I know it's wrong. The words
unsay the things I meant.

My dark girl strokes the blush across my cheek.
In the courtyard, a lizard suns itself.
The body will unsay the things it meant:
slippery husband, why won't you stay?

Ornithological Autobiography
(Audubon)

I.
In the drawing room of childhood,
the servants move docilely among the clatter
of spoons and breakfast dishes.
A violent flutter shakes the cage.
Then stillness, and green feathers
drifting upward.

The monkey was afterwards forever chained,
the parrot buried with befitting pomp,
laid in a little box with gold hinges.

II.
Who draws from a stuffed specimen knows neither
the true length, nor junction of the wings and body,
knows nothing of the creature's gait or natural allurements.

III.
I destroyed these drawings, and began again.

IV.
We glide across the frozen Perkioming,
winter darkness descending
like a kestrel wing.
Each night sleep takes me unaware until
I come up gasping from the cold
below. Gas lamps wink dimly

beyond the banks. Our skates trace
migratory patterns behind us,
illegible in the scarred ice,
in the dark of Lower Providence.

V.

For shooting I donned my black satin smallclothes
and silk stockings, the finest ruffled shirt
in Philadelphia. Helpless to my nature
as the goldfinch with his yellow cape,
the flycatcher in his blowsy cap.

VI.

I had no vices, it is true.
Temperate to an intemperate degree,
I did not taste a glass of wine until my wedding day.

VII.

I've long left the island of my birth.
On a veranda my mother brushing
her long black hair. In the trees,
the Ivory-billed Woodpecker
drilling its musketry into the hollow branches.

On that colony, the dream-hued flowers
open their long-necked blooms. *And the newly-hatched
young, no larger than humble-bees—*

Forgive me. Like the falcon with her prey,
I have dragged the story home and, bloody-beaked,
eviscerated it.

Brazil, Imaginary Island

In trees, the embers stir, birds
whose feathers flare in the dark.

At night I hear my sons whispering
in their mosquito nets. *Remember
how the leaves fell down?
Remember snow?*

The day is half light, half dark.
Thus the Spanish and the Portuguese
once split the world in two.

By the pool, the flowers droop.
The ones they call *graça*,
with their glowing throats
and feathered tongues.

Instant Message from Salvador, Bahia

Today was sunny and the beach
at Itapuá was crowded and I thought of you.
I cut my foot on the coral beneath the tide pools.

On the screen, the greenish script glitters
like the dolphin who flipped
his body up into the sun. Suddenly
appearing, then
it's gone again.

I saw the whales last week, passing through.
Their backs and haunches turning over,
like a slow thought
in the mouth of the Bay of All Saints.

Here it's dark already: austral winter.
Can you see our shadows
flit against the unlit
background? I see your sons
move in and out of the frame—
their faces older,
changed.

Do the whales make their way that far north?
Is it possible we move
in that same dark medium,
that same ponderous physical world?

The Poem I Meant to Write

It breathes among the breakfast dishes, gilled
and fickle. Gurete in the kitchen wields
a knife: a scythe of scales gathers on the floor.
"Today is your day off," she says. "Therefore
you can help clean fish." The lines
that caught my waking in their tangled twine
unreel. The poem turns a silver fin and dives
for darker water. I roll my sleeves and give
my hands to the rhythm of slit and gut.
Talk skates the mirrored surface of the skin. Gurete
laughs as words keep slipping from my grasp.
The shiny bodies split themselves in heaps: what's
useful and what's not. The thin blood
spreads and darkens. In my hands, the bones unclasp.

Firefly

In the meadow, in mid-
June, memory's cold
light flashes. My son
holds it in cupped
hands, saying, can I keep it?
Can it be my pet?

American Bittern (*Botaurus lentiginosus*)

Somewhere at the edge
of a swamp in Connecticut,
my brother is listening
to our parents'
old records.

Since our parents no longer have the means
to hear them, what remains? Hard
rain. Ophelia, where have you
gone?

It's getting dark. My brother's wife
is somewhere else, stitching up
a patient's abdomen.

There's no cure. California
tumbles into the sea. It'll
swallow you in.

Loss of habitat is one thing.
But whatever your tongue wants
you to believe, the heron isn't
acid or aggrieved, not cold
or sullen or ill-disposed.

The heron can't help
her conspicuous
flight feathers. Her dark streak.

In the unlit room, my brother
waits for the unmistakeable call,
for the angular bird to dip its beak
to the wavering
black lake.

Windows

1.
The storms that hit South Florida
are brief. Sudden flash
of clarity in the unstable
air. The only perfect memory,
the neuroscientists say, is the one
not accessed. Thus her life
perfects itself in the tousled
cumulonimbus bringing
cool air and rain
to Earth. Every afternoon
she looks out the window
and sighs, *It's been so long
since it last rained.*

2.
Entire walls are made of glass.
The table is glass. The clocks
are glass. Finally we have succeeded
in making time
invisible.

The tongue sandwich
on rye hovers
in midair.

3.
Who does he look like?
my grandmother asks, pinching
my son's cheek.
Who does he look like?

4.
Every year a billion birds die
flying into windows.
Think about their skills at flying
through tree branches and leaves.
Think how easy it is
to mistake one thing
for another.

The Vegetable Plot

Harvest: Midsummer

This is my favorite time, before
mold claims the zucchini leaves,
before the chard turns tough and sullen
and the spinach bolts. I kneel
in front of the butter lettuce,
tender heads in which I take
inordinate pride. As though
it were my tending, and not
the turning of the earth
that brings them forth. As later,
when I am tearing the leaves
for salad, calling my sons
to wash their hands, I feel
for a moment the almost weightless
syllables I have plucked, it seems now,
from air, and chosen
willfully to love.

On a Line by Petrarch

What I once loved I now love less.
September leaves us shadows
but no light. I watch you undress,

your body edged in darkness.
Miles on the stereo, those notes
that I once loved, and now love less—

the glint of anger they suppress
turns a kind of airless blue,
admits no light. I watch you undress

your gestures of significance,
and leave me at a loss to know
what I once loved. I now love less

than fluently, am forced to guess
at curve of neck and arch of brow.
But not at light. I watch you without redress

to sound or sense. The needle lifts
at last from the refrain, its echo:
What I once loved I now love less.
But no; not light; not watching you, undressed.

Crabapple (*Malus coronaria*)

My son climbs onto the roof
of the shed to shake the apples down:
little bullets pelting the grass.

Why is he so bent
on destruction, on taking things
apart?

I follow him with a bucket,
collecting the fallen fruit.

The first time he said to me,
I hate you, everything
came down like that, an ugly
clattering.

The second time, too.

So small and sour.
So bruised and complicated.

Then all the hours seething
in the kitchen, all the sugar it takes
to turn them into something
palatable, pellucid
blood-red gifts
lined up on the counter.

Ode to Bly's Translations of Neruda

Professor of the Scorched Shoe,
it is you I return to now, preparing
for the job of middle school Spanish teacher.
Because like you, I want the words to be
not *transparent*, but something *through which*
light passes. Because this is the essence of language
pedagogy, this *bodega de profundidad*, and who knows
when I will need to tell a seventh grader
the mouths suffers more
than all the toes, or *I know you will never*
believe me, but
it sings. Doctor of Solitude, this is how
I like to read you: at night, while eating a bowl
of well-salted popcorn.
Scholar of Buried Light, the salt
sings. What I want to know
is how would you translate *palomitas?*
I prefer you thus, weightless
as a feather on my tongue, split
into your two hemispheres. Having now lived
in both myself—borealis and Southern
Cross, latinate and Anglo-
Saxon, song of grief and wild rivers
of delight, I could ask, why *says* for *dreams?*
Why *goatskin* for *pellejo de oveja?* Does the
fleecy cloud of Spanish transform in English
to a species harder and more obdurate? Sometimes,

I admit, I like to recite what I remember of you
in my head, as I feed the baby goats their bottles:
The dry universe / all at once / given dark stars /
by this firmament of coolness,
as I pat their coarse flanks, light and dark,
Clara and Clementine, and lock them into the barn
with imperfect tenderness, bright stars
in the constellation Auriga.
But who else, Bard of the Broken
Voice, would see the backlit
clarity of *star-filled* in *celestial*? Who else
allow the *sabor central del infinito* to strip its sibilance
and reveal its fleshy vowels, as
the inward flavor of the infinite?
Perhaps this is why I prefer to read you
at night, the house quiet and my children
asleep. It is easy to adore them
in their stillness, their longings and their teeth
converted to cool light.

South Dakota Ghazal

In fourth grade, the answers were luminous
and whole: four, chlorophyll, South Dakota.

Plume of dust rising from an empty bowl—
the last they saw of South Dakota.

The fields of Normandy during the war
reminded him of nothing so much as South Dakota.

Each geography repeats another. The heart a sovereign
nation beneath a sternum flat as South Dakota.

August 1804: Lewis and Clark enter
the Garden of Eden, or South Dakota.

Don't mistake the spruce for its blue-green
needles, or these lines for a map of South Dakota.

Barking squirrels and burning river bluffs;
Buffalo, Clear Lake, Bonesteel: South Dakota.

The sun knocked on our tent in Vermillion and tugged us
toward Rapid City, the tumbledown edge of South Dakota.

The first winter he slept in a cave he dug with his hands.
Its earth embrace the only thing that held him in South Dakota.

The Oglala say stones are the oldest people. But it was white men
who carved their own ancestries into the hills of South Dakota.

It's what names do. This one my parents gave me, *El*,
it puts corners around me square as South Dakota.

Two Common Daffodils
(*Narcissus pseudonarcissus*)

> *Oh hours of childhood, when behind each shape*
> *more than the past appeared, / and what streamed*
> *out before us was not the future.*
>
> —Rilke, "The Fourth Elegy"

I ride backwards on the train, facing where I'm coming from,
      gritty town
of numbered streets, March with its muddy footprints, saying,
not so fast. The book on my lap illuminated in the window.
      Rilke
spread ghostly over the chemical plants of North Jersey, over
      the smoke
cocooning in the sky and disappearing. Rilke
and his adolescent longing no one leaves behind, except
in longing more.

We fought before I left. Now, the boys in bed,
you pour cachaça in a glass. Crush the ice
and lime, stir in the sugar with a knife.

Each intensifies the other—lime's bruised peel,
sugar echoing the ice's hard clarity.

The pleasure's in not yielding.

The light is slipping from the loading docks
and storage lockers, behind the pawnshops and the strip clubs.
You enter our sons' room
to watch them sleeping. Mouths agape, limbs entwined.
On the dresser, in a tin can's makeshift vase, the flowers
I picked earlier, their bells drooping.

In the living room, you slip your parents' old record
from its sleeve. Stan Getz in his yellow starched lapels,
the saxophone's brass slouch. Even though it's dark,
I know these last few miles: marsh grass and mud,
and the long tunnel. You lower the needle. What streams out
is gently tongued regret, so many variations on a single note.

Parsnips

Late sown, they grow
thrifty; in this narrow
rowhouse kitchen,
we set their two-pronged
hearts in jars of water
on the windowsill.
We have little sun,
less earth, and yet
I want my sons to know
that what feeds them
grows from light.

The River Trail

I'm held by nothing, I hold on to nothing, I belong to nothing.

Driving home early from the party
to relieve the babysitter, the city
is so many lights blinking goodbye.

And boathouse row, the houses lit up in outline
like a child's drawing of houses.

Should we have surrendered sooner
to the suburbs' silent pull, their slow
oar stroke, glide and lull?

Along the river, the sculls are stacked
against the walls, long-bodied mantises.

Held by nothing but West River's
centripetal tug, we pass a late-season
carnival. So far from my own childhood,
the moon bounce hovers.

A woman holds her grease crayon poised
above a child's cheek. An orange popsicle
trickles its fluorescence down the child's arm.

And my own sons—I see them
slipping off their shoes,
climbing into the netted inflatable world.

Driving to the Shore with My Father

The pine barrens in early morning darkness: a raccoon
slinks off into the staggerbush, the carnivorous
plants. Mid-August, the descent begun.

The water's like that too. Folding itself into the invisible.
Its gray blade honed on the coming storm.

The fronts that pass over him are brief
and devastating. They scatter their debris
across my childhood.

At the turnaround, the empty Café Atlantis glows:
Open 24 Hours. The chrome counter,
the same pies rotating under glass, spotlit.

We are both more clever than compassionate.

Also: pigheaded and practical, believing above all
in work's salvation.

Soon enough sunlight's cleaver coming down hard
on the tarmac. We follow the signs
for Long Beach Island. Keep right. Yield.

Invention for Cavaquinho
and Pedal Steel

October's glint is mordent, already long in the tooth.
      Ornamental kale
all that's left in the garden. Study is useless. For forty years
my father's fingers have stumbled over the same notes on the piano.

      Wednesday nights we take up our instruments. Jew's harp,
lyre, pedal steel. The gourds that swelled all summer and dried up.
Ezra, awake past bedtime in his houndstooth suit,
strums his small guitar and sings. We play from memory.

At twelve I ran through the woods
in racing flats, memorizing momentum, how it took me
down the hills and then back up, mud-splattered quarter notes
on my calves.

At twenty, I sat on a flat cement roof, the hill a sharp
mile above the sea, shelling peas. The parched earth, steep ravines,
clouds passing below us. Girl whetting a machete. Man knocking
      out a beat
on a Fanta bottle's ribs. And the bones visible through my skin,
elbow's tuning peg, clavicle's awkward ornament.

Memory practices on us: mortar, pestle, fire kindled
in the wrist's stone cup. Celestial storehouse, where the boxes
of yellowed photos pile up—

The years of lessons, practice sheets filled in, initialed.
My flute in its black case, banging against my knees.
I learned to mime the stops: sleeves of my white shirt raised,
close together, the way a moth lands, with its wings closed.

I was such a serious child.

Whatever hour the school bus left us at the corner, late fall,
dark falling, we found my mother on her knees,
spade in hand, turning the soil. The white fence posts
glowed. Spirit burial ground, where under leaf cover, the worms
move like silent tongues, compost's shadow notes,
diminuendo.

Invention of the Moon

By the Sea of Crisis, I lay out my thin towel. Behind me,
the bright roiling city, the stands selling beer and coconuts.
Women in white dresses kneel to wash the church steps.
Carnaval music pulses from the speakers. The beat is blunt
as the dull knife a drunk

        plunges into another's ribcage.

But the ocean's grace notes—mordent, descending
appoggiatura—pull me under.

Sea of Nectar. Sea of the Edge. This is how the days
repeat themselves, rolling over. Life, as someone said
of the Bach Inventions, is "clearly impossible to execute

       at any reasonable tempo."

This is the year I don't sleep, but instead follow the moon's light-
suffused motif—augmentation, diminution.

                The Mare Desiderii,
the Sea of Dreams, was long ago declared a fallacy.

I pick up the easy badinage, the greetings
and the curses. But for my youngest
son, it's all he has. He points at the waxing gibbous
and says,

          lua.

Letter to Laura from Arembepe

In the thatch-roofed Hippy Village, the man is hacking open
a coconut. He drops a straw into the jagged hole. The smooth
white flesh, cup like an inverted moon.

Once Janis Joplin stayed here, slept in a hammock strung
between two palms; threw herself into the rough
surf, or lay floating on her back and stared at clear blue sky.

       There it's getting cold again. Again,
the heartbeat on the screen grew faint
and flickered out. When you told me, your voice broke.
I didn't know if it was the weight of loss, or just the miles
of ocean the cable's buried under.

       Here the shore's bicornuate: split
along rocks' ventricle. The shallows where the children play,
the churning on the other side.

I hold my sons' small hands, and we wade in.
Even in the glassy calm, I feel the undertow,
ocean's umbilical pull.
       My boys slip
beyond my grasp, their bodies slick as seals.

       And Janis rises up beyond the sharp outcropping,
her hair wild, the woody shell of her voice
cracking, the sweet water spilling out.

Itapuã: Footnotes

1 The coconut vendor with his machete and his dirty rag.
Amiga, he calls me.

2 The surfers know the invisible rocks beneath the water.

3 In the interior, the doors to the houses are always open.

4 The men play a game with little stones: drop one in each
smooth indentation.

5 Meningitis. Dengue. The voice on the line that says, we have
your son.

6 The future subjunctive: *Se Deus quiser.*

7 In the middle of the road there was a stone.

8 a terrible necessity

9 small, red-orange fruit, firm-fleshed, acidic.

10 In the year 1500, Cabral found himself, quite by accident, in
Brazil.

11 There was a stone in the middle of the road.

12 Believing the newly discovered land to be an island he gave it the name Island of the True Cross and took possession of it.

13 One spits out the large stone.

14 It's a stick, it's a stone, it's the end of the road . . .

Domestic

She snaps the linens square.
A field of flax: glaucous green,
slender lanceolate,
unspun. She crossed the border
lying on a raft. Perhaps
her eyes were shut. Perhaps
staring at the muddy sky.

Aguas de Março: Midwestern Reprise

It's a birch, it's a stone, it's the end
of the road. It's the gray of the sky,
it's the melt in the lake. It's the mud,
it's the mud. . . . It's the pulse
in the wrist, it's the sliced hearts
of palm, it's the claim that you stake
with your knife and your fork.
It's the body in bed, it's the smooth
of the sheet. It's the morning that breaks
in a flurry of doves. It's the waking
of yeast, it's the dough, it's the knead.
It's the rise and the rest.
It's the rise in the creek
and the rise in the chest. It's the need,
it's the need. It's the bridge,
it's the pass, it's the hook
and the line. It's the fish and the thrash,
it's the late squall of snow. It's the mud,
it's the mud. . . . It's the shut
hatch of spring, it's your key in the door.
It's the cracking of floes and the breaking
of codes, it's the finch on the branch,
it's the nest in the eaves. It's the waking
from sleep, it's the creak and the groan,

it's the crocus, the frog, it's the ravenous
bear. It's the promise of warmth, it's
a promise to stay, it's the will,
it's the won't, it's the leak in the roof.
It's the mud, it's the mud . . .

Weaning

Sweat stood at attention
on the prow of his nose.

It was still: windless.

This thin rope tossed out
to the drowning.

And the Lehigh rising,
carrying the little leaf-boats
down.

Previous titles in the Carnegie Mellon Poetry Series

The Autobiography of a Jukebox, Cornelius Eady
The Patience of the Cloud Photographer, Elizabeth Holmes
Madly in Love, Aliki Barnstone
An Octave Above Thunder: New and Selected Poems, Carol Muske

1998
Yesterday Had a Man in It, Leslie Adrienne Miller
Definition of the Soul, John Skoyles
Dithyrambs, Richard Katrovas
Postal Routes, Elizabeth Kirschner
The Blue Salvages, Wayne Dodd
The Joy Addict, James Harms
Clemency and Other Poems, Colette Inez
Scattering the Ashes, Jeff Friedman
Sacred Conversations, Peter Cooley
Life Among the Trolls, Maura Stanton

1999
Justice, Caroline Finkelstein
Edge of House, Dzvinia Orlowsky
A Thousand Friends of Rain: New and Selected Poems, 1976-1998, Kim Stafford
The Devil's Child, Fleda Brown Jackson
World as Dictionary, Jesse Lee Kercheval
Vereda Tropical, Ricardo Pau-Llosa
The Museum of the Revolution, Angela Ball
Our Master Plan, Dara Wier

2000
Small Boat with Oars of Different Size, Thom Ward
Post Meridian, Mary Ruefle
Hierarchies of Rue, Roger Sauls
Constant Longing, Dennis Sampson
Mortal Education, Joyce Peseroff
How Things Are, James Richardson
Years Later, Gregory Djanikian
On the Waterbed They Sank to Their Own Levels, Sarah Rosenblatt
Blue Jesus, Jim Daniels
Winter Morning Walks: 100 Postcards to Jim Harrison, Ted Kooser

2001
Day Moon, Jon Anderson
The Origin of Green, T. Alan Broughton
Lovers in the Used World, Gillian Conoley
Quarters, James Harms
Mastodon, 80% Complete, Jonathan Johnson
The Deepest Part of the River, Mekeel McBride
Earthly, Michael McFee
Ten Thousand Good Mornings, James Reiss
The World's Last Night, Margot Schilpp
Sex Lives of the Poor and Obscure, David Schloss
Glacier Wine, Maura Stanton
Voyages in English, Dara Wier

2002
Keeping Time, Suzanne Cleary
Astronaut, Brian Henry
What It Wasn't, Laura Kasischke
Slow Risen Among the Smoke Trees, Elizabeth Kirschner
The Finger Bone, Kevin Prufer
Among the Musk Ox People, Mary Ruefle
The Late World, Arthur Smith

2003
Trouble, Mary Baine Campbell
A Place Made of Starlight, Peter Cooley
Taking Down the Angel, Jeff Friedman
Lives of Water, John Hoppenthaler
Imitation of Life, Allison Joseph
Except for One Obscene Brushstroke, Dzvinia Orlowsky
The Mastery Impulse, Ricardo Pau-Llosa
Casino of the Sun, Jerry Williams

2004
The Women Who Loved Elvis All Their Lives, Fleda Brown
The Chronic Liar Buys a Canary, Elizabeth Edwards
Freeways and Aqueducts, James Harms
Prague Winter, Richard Katrovas

Anticipate the Coming Reservoir, John Hoppenthaler
Convertible Night, Flurry of Stones, Dzvinia Orlowsky
Parable Hunter, Ricardo Pau-Llosa
The Book of Sleep, Eleanor Stanford

2009
Divine Margins, Peter Cooley
Cultural Studies, Kevin A. González
Dear Apocalypse, K. A. Hays
Warhol-o-rama, Peter Oresick
Cave of the Yellow Volkswagen, Maureen Seaton
Group Portrait from Hell, David Schloss
Birdwatching in Wartime, Jeffrey Thomson

2010
The Diminishing House, Nicky Beer
A World Remembered, T. Alan Broughton
Say Sand, Daniel Coudriet
Knock Knock, Heather Hartley
In the Land We Imagined Ourselves, Jonathan Johnson
Selected Early Poems: 1958-1983, Greg Kuzma
The Other Life: Selected Poems, Herbert Scott
Admission, Jerry Williams

2011
Having a Little Talk with Capital P Poetry, Jim Daniels
Oz, Nancy Eimers
Working in Flour, Jeff Friedman
Scorpio Rising: Selected Poems, Richard Katrovas
The Politics, Benjamin Paloff
Copperhead, Rachel Richardson

2012
Now Make an Altar, Amy Beeder
Still Some Cake, James Cummins
Comet Scar, James Harms
Early Creatures, Native Gods, K. A. Hays
That Was Oasis, Michael McFee